A Condensation from
the Book

How to Win Friends
and Influence People

DALE CARNEGIE

"The ability to deal with people is as purchasable a commodity as sugar or coffee! And I will pay more for that ability than for any other under the sun."

—JOHN D. ROCKEFELLER, SR.

CONTENTS

THIS is a working handbook in human relations. It isn't merely to be read. It is to be used. If the knowledge it contains isn't applied, it will soon be forgotten.

Why not carry this booklet in your pocket every day?

Why not read it before you have that difficult interview?

Why not review it before you dictate that touchy letter?

Why not glance at it every time you are tempted to criticize or complain or talk about what you want?

How to Win Friends and Influence People

1. Don't Criticize

The German army won't let a soldier file a complaint and make a criticism immediately after a thing has happened. He has to sleep on his grudge first and cool off. If he files his complaint immediately, he is punished. By the eternals, there ought to be a law like that in civil life too—a law for whining parents and nagging wives and scolding employers and the whole obnoxious parade of fault-finders. If you want to gather honey, don't go around "kicking over bee-hives," as Abe Lincoln used to put it. The late John Wanamaker once confessed: "I learned thirty years ago that it is foolish to scold. I have enough trouble overcoming my own limitations without fretting over the fact that God has not seen fit to distribute evenly the gift of intelligence." Wanamaker learned this lesson early; but I personally had to live in this old world for a third of a century before it even began to dawn upon me that ninety-nine times out of a hundred, no man ever criticizes himself for anything, no matter how wrong he may be. When dealing with people, let us remember that we are not dealing with creatures of logic. We are dealing with beings of emotion, human beings bristling with prejudices and motivated by pride and vanity. Criticism is futile because it puts a man on the defensive and usually makes him strive to justify himself, no matter how wrong he may be. Criticism is dangerous because it wounds a man's precious pride, hurts his sense of importance and arouses his resentment. "I never criticize anyone," says Mr. Schwab. "I am anxious to praise but loath to find fault." Do you know someone you would like to change and regulate and improve? Good! That is fine. Why not begin on yourself? From a purely selfish standpoint, that is a lot more profitable than trying to improve others—and a lot less dangerous. It will probably take from now until Christmas to perfect yourself. You can then have a nice long rest over the holidays and devote the New Year to criticizing other people. But perfect yourself first. "Don't complain about the snow on your neighbor's roof," said Confucius, "when your own doorstep is unclean." Any fool can criticize, condemn and complain— and most fools do. But it takes character and self-control to be understanding and forgiving. "A great man shows his greatness," said Carlyle, "by the way he treats little men." When Mrs. Lincoln condemned the Southerners during the Civil War, Lincoln, with malice towards none and charity for all, said to her: "Don't criticize them. They are just what we would be under similar circumstances." Instead of condemning people, let's try to understand them. Let's try to figure out *why* they do what they do. That's a lot more profitable and far more intriguing than criticism; and it breeds sympathy, tolerance, and kindness. "To know all is to forgive all." The brilliant Dr. Johnson once remarked: "God Himself, sir, does not propose to judge man until the end of his days." Why then should you and I?

2. Give Honest Appreciation

I once interviewed the only man in the world who was ever paid a straight salary of a million dollars a year—Charles Schwab. Andrew Carnegie paid Mr. Schwab a million dollars a year. For what? For Schwab's knowledge of steel? No. Schwab himself told me it was largely because of his skill in human relationships. So I asked Mr. Schwab to reveal to me the secret of his extraordinary ability to deal with people. Here it is in his own words—words that ought to be cast in eternal bronze and hung in every home and school, in every shop and office in the land—words that children ought to memorize instead of wasting their time memorizing the declension of Latin verbs or the amount of annual rainfall in Brazil—words that will all but transform your life and mine if we will only live them: "I consider my ability to arouse enthusiasm among the men," said Mr. Schwab, "the greatest asset I possess, and the way to develop the best that is in a man is by appreciation and encouragement. There is nothing else that so quickly kills the ambitions of a man as criticisms from his superiors. I never criticize anyone. I believe in giving a man an incentive to work. So I am anxious to praise but loath to find fault. If I like anything, I am hearty in my approbation and lavish in my praise."

That is what Schwab does. But what does the average man do? The exact opposite. If he doesn't like a thing, he raises the old Harry; if he does like it, he says nothing. Abraham Lincoln began one of his letters by saying: "Everyone likes a compliment . . ." Yes, of course, we do. Professor John Dewey, America's most profound philosopher, declares that the deepest urge in human nature is "the desire to be important." And compliments make us feel important.

We all crave appreciation, we all long for sincere praise—and we seldom get either. Here is a gnawing and unfaltering human hunger, and the man who honestly satisfies it will hold people in the palm of his hand. Flattery? No! No! Flattery is shallow, selfish and insincere. It ought to fail, and it usually does. Flattery is from the teeth out. Sincere appreciation is from the heart out. No! No! No! I am not suggesting flattery! Far from it. I'm talking about a new way of life. Let me repeat. I am talking about a new way of life. "In my wide association in life, meeting with many and great men in various parts of the world," Schwab declared, "I have yet to find the man, however great or exalted his station, who did not do better work and put forth greater effort under a spirit of approval than he would ever do under a spirit of criticism."

That he said, frankly, was one of the outstanding reasons for the phenomenal success of Andrew Carnegie. Carnegie praised his associates publicly as well as privately. Carnegie wanted to praise his assistants even on his tombstone. He wrote an epitaph for himself which read: "Here lies one who knew how to get around him men who were cleverer than himself."

3. Don't Talk About What You Want; Talk About What Your Listener Wants

I like strawberries and cream; but when I went fishing up in Maine last summer, I didn't bait the hook with strawberries and cream. I didn't bait the hook with what I liked. I baited it with what the fish liked. Why don't you and I use the same common sense when fishing for men? You are intensely and eternally interested in what you want. But no one else is. The rest of us are just like you: we are interested in what we want. So the only way on earth to influence the other fellow is to talk about what he wants and show him how to get it. Remember that tomorrow when you are trying to get somebody to do something. If, for example, you don't want your son to smoke, don't preach to him from your point of view, but show him that cigarettes may keep him from making the baseball team or winning the hundred-yard dash. Ralph Waldo Emerson told in his Journal how he and his son tried to get a rebellious calf into the barn. Emerson pushed and his son pulled; but the calf stiffened his legs and stubbornly resisted. The Irish housemaid saw their predicament, put a maternal finger in the calf's mouth, and let the calf suck her finger as she gently led him into the barn. Emerson had thought only of what he wanted; but the Irish maid thought of what the calf wanted. "If there is any one secret of success," says Henry Ford, "it lies in the ability to get the other person's point of view and see things from his angle as well as from your own."

Five Ways to Make People Like You

1. Become Genuinely Interested in Other People

Many of the sweetest memories of my child-hood cluster around a little yellow-haired dog with a stub tail. "Tippy" never read a book on psychology. He didn't need to. Neither Professor William James nor Professor Har-ry Overstreet could have told him anything about human relationships. He had a perfect technique for making people like him. He liked people himself—and his interest in me was so sincere and so genuine that I couldn't keep from liking him and loving him in return. Do you want to make friends? Then take a tip from "Tippy." Be friend-ly. Forget yourself. Think of others. "Tippy" knew that you can make more friends in two months by becoming genu-inely interested in other people than you can in two years by trying to get other people in-terested in you. Let me repeat that. This time, I'll italicize it. *You can make more friends in two months by becoming interested in other people than you can in two years by trying to get other people interested in you.* Yet I know and you know people who blun-der through life trying to wigwag other peo-

19

ple into becoming interested in them.

Of course, it doesn't work. People are not interested in you. They are not interested in me. They are interested in themselves—morning, noon, and after dinner. The New York Telephone Company made a detailed study of telephone conversations to find out which word is the most frequently used. You have guessed it: it is the personal pronoun "I." "I." "I." It was used 3990 times in 500 telephone conversations. "I." "I." "I." "I." "I." When you see a group photograph that you are in, whose picture do you look for first? If you think people are interested in you, answer this question: If you died tonight, how many people would come to your funeral? Why should people be interested in you unless you are first interested in them? Reach for your pencil now and write your reply here:

If we merely try to impress people and get people interested in us, we will never have many true, sincere friends. Friends, real friends, are not made that way. Napoleon tried it; and in his last meeting with Josephine, he said: "Josephine, I have been as fortunate as any man ever was on this earth; and yet, at this hour, you are the only person in the world on whom I can rely." And historians doubt whether he could rely on even her.

Hudson Maxim, the inventor of smokeless powder, gave some very sound advice when he said: "There are two kinds of consideration people seek to achieve from others, admiration and love. Now the way you want to conduct yourself is to let admiration go hang and get people to love you. Whenever people admire, they envy, and envy makes enemies." Let me repeat: *"You can make more friends in two months by becoming genuinely interested in other people than you can in two years by trying to get other people interested in you."*

2. Smile

I attended a dinner party one night at the Casino in Central Park. One of the guests, a woman who had inherited money, was eager to make a pleasing impression on everyone. She had spent a modest fortune on sables, diamonds and pearls. But she hadn't done anything whatever about her face. It radiated sourness and selfishness. She didn't realize that the expression she wore on her face was more important than the clothes she wore on her back. Charles Schwab said his smile had been worth a million dollars. And he was probably understating the truth. I once spent an hour with Maurice Chevalier. He was glum and taciturn—sharply different from what I expected—until he smiled. Then it seemed as if the sun had broken through a cloud. If it hadn't been for his smile, Maurice Chevalier would probably still be a cabinet-maker back in Paris, following the trade of his father and brothers.

A smile radiates warmth. It says, "I'm glad to see you. You make me happy." Well, if you are genuinely glad to see me, I am certainly going to be glad to see you. An insincere grin? No. That doesn't fool anybody. We know it is mechanical and we resent it. I am talking about a real smile, a heart-warming smile, a smile that comes from within. How can you get yourself into the habit of smiling? Listen to this. Professor William James of Harvard said: "Action seems to follow feeling, but really action and feeling go together . . . Thus the sovereign voluntary path to cheerfulness is to sit up cheerfully and to act and speak as if cheerfulness were already there."

3. Remember That a Man's Name Is to Him the Sweetest and Most Important Sound in the English Language

I once asked Jim Farley to tell me the secret of his success. He said, "Hard work," and I said, "Don't be funny." He then asked me what I thought was the reason for his success. I replied: "I understand you can call ten thousand people by their first names." "No. You are wrong," he said. "I can call fifty thousand people by their first names." Make no mistake about it. That ability helped Jim Farley put Franklin D. Roosevelt in the White House. I recently conducted a course for the Junior League of New York, and one of the young women said she had discovered early in life how to be popular at a dance. She managed to get a young man's name the first time he danced with her; and when he cut in again later in the evening, she called his name and called it with enthusiasm. He was hers, after that, for the rest of the evening. We frequently have difficulty in remembering the names of people to whom we have been introduced because we never heard the name clearly. If you don't understand a man's name, you can pay him a very fine tribute by saying: "I am so sorry. I didn't get the name clearly." He will be pleased to think you have attached so much importance to his name. Ask him to repeat it. Ask him to spell it. If it is an unusual name, remark how unusual it is. And while you are talking to him, keep saying his name over and over in your mind. Use his name several times in your conversation and when you say goodbye, repeat his name again.

4. Be a Good Listener. Encourage Others to Talk about Themselves

I was recently invited to a bridge party. Personally, I don't play bridge; and there was a young woman there—and she didn't play bridge either. She had discovered that my professional work had made it necessary for me to travel in Europe for about five years. So she said: "Oh, Mr. Carnegie, I do want you to tell me about all the wonderful places you have visited and the sights you have seen." As we sat down on the sofa, she remarked that she and her husband had recently returned from a trip to Africa. So I said: "How interesting. Did you visit the big game country? Do tell me about Africa. I have always wanted to see it." That was good for forty-five minutes. She never again asked me where I had been or what I had seen. She didn't want to hear me talk about my travels. All she wanted was an interested listener so she could expand her ego and tell about where she had been. Was she unusual? No. Most of us are like that. So if you aspire to be a good conversationalist, be an interested listener. Ask questions that the other man will enjoy answering. Encourage him to talk about himself and his accomplishments. Remember that the man you are talking to is a hundred times more interested in himself and his wants and his problems than he is in you and your problems. His toothache means more to him than a famine in China that kills a million people. A boil on his neck interests him more than forty earthquakes in Africa. Think of that the next time you start a conversation.

5. Make the Other Person Feel Important— and Do It Sincerely

There is one all-important law of human conduct. If we obey that law, we will seldom get into trouble. But if we break it, we will get into endless trouble. The law is this: Always make the other person feel important. Professor John Dewey, as we have already noted, says that the desire to be important is the deepest urge in human nature. It is the urge that differentiates us from the animals. It is the urge that has been responsible for civilization itself. Philosophers have been speculating on the riles of human relationships for thousands of years; and out of all that speculation, there has evolved only one important precept. It is not new. Zoroaster taught it to his fire-worshippers in Persia three thousand years ago. Confucius preached it in China twenty-four centuries ago. Lao-Tsze, the founder of Taoism, taught it to his followers in the Valley of the Han. Buddha preached it on the banks of the Ganges five hundred years before Christ. The sacred books of Hinduism taught it a thousand years before that. Jesus taught it among the hills of Judea nineteen centuries ago. Jesus summed it up in one sentence—probably the most important sentence in the world—"Do unto others as you would have others do unto you." You want the approval of those with whom you come in contact. You want recognition of your true worth. You want a feeling that you are important in your little world. You don't want to listen to cheap, insincere flattery; but you do crave sincere appreciation. You want your friends and associates to be, as Charles Schwab puts it, "hearty in their approbation and lavish in their praise." All of us want that. So let's obey the Golden Rule, and give unto others what we would have others give unto us. I once succumbed to the fad of fasting and went six days and nights without eating anything whatever. It wasn't difficult. I was less hungry at the end of the sixth day than I was at the end of the second. Yet I know people who would think they had committed a crime if they let their families or employees go for six days without food; but they will let them go for six days and six weeks, and sometimes sixty years, without giving them the hearty appreciation, the recognition, the sincere praise, that they crave as much as they crave food. Reading this won't do you any good unless you apply it. Begin at once. Where? Why not begin at home? Dorothy Dix, an expert on the causes of marital infelicity, says: "Praising a woman before marriage is a matter of inclination. But praising one after you marry her is a matter of necessity and personal safety. Matrimony is no place for candor. It is a field for diplomacy. If you wish to fare sumptuously every day, never knock your wife's housekeeping or make invidious comparisons between it and your mother's. But, on the contrary, be forever praising her domesticity and openly congratulate yourself upon having married the only woman who combines the attractions of Venus and Minerva and Mary Ann. Even when the steak is leather and the

bread a cinder, don't complain. Merely remark that the meal isn't up to her usual stan-
dard of perfection, and she will make a burnt
offering of herself on the kitchen stove to live
up to your ideal of her."

Nine Ways to Help Win People to Your Way of Thinking

RULE ONE—*The Only Way to Get the Best of an Argument Is to Avoid It*

During my youth, I argued with my brother about everything. When I went to college, I studied logic and argumentation and went in for debating contests. Talk about being from Missouri, I was born there. I had to be shown. Later, I taught debating and argumentation in New York and once planned to write a book on the subject. Since then, I have listened to, criticized, engaged in and watched the effects of thousands of arguments in business and social life. As a result of it all, I have come to the conclusion that it is all sheer futility and that there is only one way under high Heaven to get the best of an argument—and that is to avoid it. Nine times out of ten, an argument ends with each of the contestants being more firmly convinced than ever that he is absolutely right. You can't win an argument. You can't because if you lose it, you lose it; and if you win it, you lose it. Why? Well, suppose you triumph over the other man and shoot his argument full of holes and prove that he is *non coin pos mentis.* Then what? You will feel fine. But what about him? You have made him feel inferior. You have stirred up his resentment. The Penn Mutual Life Insurance Company has laid down a definite policy for its salesmen: "Don't argue!" Real salesmanship isn't argument. It isn't anything even remotely like argument. The human mind isn't changed that way. As wise old Ben Franklin used to say: "If you argue and rankle and contradict, you may achieve a victory sometimes; but it will be an empty victory because you will never get your opponent's good will."

RULE TWO—*Show Respect for the Other Person's Opinions; Never Tell a Man He Is Wrong*

During the last twenty-five years I have heard thousands of businessmen try to win other people to their way of thinking. And many failed because they began by saying, "I'm going to *prove* to you…"

That's bad. That's tantamount to saying: "I'm smarter than you are. I'm going to tell you a thing or two and make you change your mind!" What effect does that have on the listener? It's a challenge. It arouses opposition. It makes the speaker feel superior; but it makes the listener feel inferior. And he resents it. "So you're going to *prove* something to me, are you?" he says to himself, "Well, let's see you do it." You have made him want to battle with you before you start.

It is difficult, under even the most benign conditions, to change people's minds. So why make it harder? Why handicap yourself? If you are going to prove anything, don't let anybody know it. Do it so subtly, so adroitly that no one will feel that you are doing it.

"Men must be taught as if you taught them not, and things unknown proposed as things forgot."

So never tell a person he is wrong. Never tell him by word or gesture or look or intonation. That is true when you are dealing with men. And . . . when you are dealing with women!!! Theodore Roosevelt said when he was in the White House that if he could be right 75% of the time, he would reach the highest measure of his expectations. How often are you right? If you could depend upon being right 55% of the time, you could make a million a day in Wall Street.

If 75% was Theodore Roosevelt's highest batting average, yours is probably far less. So what right have you to assume that people who differ with you are wrong? If a man makes a statement that you know is wrong, isn't it better to begin by saying: "I may be wrong. I frequently am. Let's examine the facts." Those are magical words, "I may be wrong. I frequently am. Let's examine the facts." That is what a scientist does. Steffanson, the Arctic explorer, once said to me, "A scientist never tries to prove anything. He attempts only to find the facts." You like to be scientific in your thinking, don't you? Well, no one is stopping you but yourself. You will never get into trouble by admitting that you may be wrong. That will stop all argument and inspire the other fellow to be just as fair and open and broadminded as you are. It will make him want to admit that he, too, may be wrong. The Chinese have a proverb pregnant with the age-old wisdom of the changeless East: "He who treads softly goes far." "We sometimes find ourselves changing our minds without any resistance or heavy emotion," said Professor James Harvey Robinson, "but if we are told we are wrong we resent the imputation and harden our hearts. . . We like to continue to believe what we have been accustomed to accept as true, and the resentment aroused when doubt is cast upon any of our assumptions leads us to seek every manner of excuse for clinging to it. The result is that most of our so-called reasoning consists in finding arguments for going on believing as we already do."

RULE THREE—*If You Are Wrong, Admit It Quickly and Emphatically*

When you make a mistake, admit it with enthusiasm. It is always easier to criticize oneself than to bear condemnation from other lips. So say about yourself all the derogatory things you know the other person intends to say—and say them before he has a chance to say them—and you take the wind out of his sails. The chances are a hundred to one then that he will take a generous, forgiving attitude and minimize your mistakes. When we are wrong—and that will be surprisingly often, if we are honest with ourselves—let's admit our mistakes quickly and with enthusiasm.

That technique will not only produce astonishing results; but believe it or not, it is a lot more fun, under the circumstances, than trying to defend one's self. Any fool can try to defend his mistakes—and most fools do—but it raises one above the herd and gives one a feeling of nobility and exaltation to admit one's mistakes. One of the most beautiful things that history records about Robert E. Lee is the way he blamed himself for the failure of Pickett's charge at Gettysburg. Alibis? Oh, yes, he could have found a score. Blame others? Yes, he could have done that, for some of his division commanders had failed him. The cavalry hadn't arrived in time to support the infantry attack. But Lee was far too noble to blame others. As Pickett's beaten and bloody troops struggled back to the Confederate lines, Robert E. Lee rode out to meet them all alone and greeted them with a self-condemnation that was little short of sublime. "All this has been my fault," he confessed. "I and I alone have lost this battle."

RULE FOUR—*Begin in a Friendly Way*

If your temper is aroused and you tell 'em a thing or two, you will have a fine time unloading your feelings. But what about the other fellow? Will he share your pleasure? Will your belligerent tones, your hostile attitude, make it easy for him to agree with you? "If you come at me with your fists doubled," said Woodrow Wilson, "I think I can promise you that mine will double as fast as yours; but if you come to me and say, 'Let us sit down and take counsel together, and if we differ from one another, understand why it is that we differ from one another, just what the points at issue are,' we will presently find that we are not so far apart after all, that the points on which we differ are few and the points on which we agree are many, and that if we only have the patience and the candor and the desire to get together, we will get together." Charles Schwab was passing through one of his steel mills one day at noon when he came across some of his employees smoking. Immediately above their heads was a sign which said, "No smoking." Did Schwab point to the sign and say, "Can't you read?" Oh no, not Schwab. He walked over to the men, handed each one a cigar and said, "I'll appreciate it, boys, if you will smoke these on the outside." They knew that he knew that they had broken a rule—and they admired him because he said nothing about it and gave them a little present and made them feel important. Couldn't keep from loving a man like that, could you?

RULE FIVE—*Get the Other Person Saying*

"Yes-Yes" Immediately

Don't begin by talking about the things on which you differ. Begin by emphasizing—and keep on emphasizing—the things on which you agree. Keep emphasizing—if possible—that you are both striving for the same end and your only difference is one of method and not of purpose. Get the other person saying "Yes-Yes" at the outset. Keep him, if possible, from saying "No."

"A 'No' response," says Professor Overstreet in his book, *Influencing Human Behavior,* "is a most difficult handicap to overcome. When a person has said 'No,' all his pride of personality demands that he remain consistent with himself. He may later feel that the 'No' was ill-advised; nevertheless, there is his precious pride to consider! Once having said a thing, he must stick to it. Hence it is of the very greatest importance that we start a person in the affirmative direction. Get a student to say 'No' at the beginning, or a customer, child, husband, or wife, and it takes the wisdom and the patience of angels to transform that bristling negative into an affirmative." Socrates made some silly mistakes. For example, he married a girl of eighteen when he was bald-headed and forty. Yet he exercised a profound influence upon the history of human thought. His magic method was to ask a series of questions which compelled the other person to answer "Yes-Yes." An excellent technique. Why not try it?

RULE SIX—*Let the Other Man Do a Great Deal of the Talking*

Most people, when trying to win others to their way of thinking, do too much talking themselves. Salesmen, especially, are guilty of this costly error. Let the other man talk himself out. He knows more about his business and his problems than you do. So ask him questions. Let him tell you a few things. If you disagree with him, you may be tempted to interrupt. But don't. It is dangerous. He won't pay attention to you while he still has a lot of ideas of his own crying for expression. So listen patiently and with an open mind. Be sincere about it. Encourage him to express his ideas fully. Isaac F. Marcosson, who is probably the world's champion interviewer of celebrities, declared that many people fail to make a favorable impression because they don't listen attentively. "They have been so much concerned with what they are going to say next that they do not keep their ears open... Big men have told me that they prefer good listeners to good talkers, but the ability to listen seems rarer than almost any other good trait." And not only big men crave a good listener, but ordinary folk do too. As the Reader's Digest once said: "Many persons call a doctor when all they want is an audience." So let's be a good audience to the other chap; and when he finishes, he will probably be encouraged by our attitude to be a good audience for our side of the story.

RULE SEVEN—*Try Honestly to See Things from the Other Person's Point of View*

Remember that the other man may be totally wrong. But he doesn't think so. Don't condemn him. Any fool can do that. Try to understand him. Only wise, tolerant, exceptional men even try to do that. There is a reason why the other man thinks and acts as he does. Ferret out that hidden reason—and you have the key to his actions—perhaps to his personality. Try honestly to put yourself in his place.

If you say to yourself, "How would I feel, how would I react if I were in his shoes," you will save a lot of time and irritation, and you will sharply increase your skill in human relationships. Dean Donham of the Harvard Business School once remarked: "I would rather walk the sidewalk in front of a man's office for two hours before an interview than step into his office without a perfectly clear idea of what I am going to say and what he—from my knowledge of his interests and motives—is likely to answer." If, as a result of reading this booklet, you get only one thing: an increased tendency to think always in terms of the other person's point of view and see things from his angle as well as your own—if you get only that one thing from this booklet, it may easily prove to be one of the milestones of your career.

RULE EIGHT—*Let the Other Man Feel That the Idea Is His*

Miss Ida Tarbell told me that she once interviewed an assistant to Owen D. Young—a man who had sat in the same office with Mr. Young for years. This man said he had never heard Owen D. Young give a direct order to anyone. "What do you think of this idea?" Mr. Young would ask; or, "Do you think this would work?" and so on.

Don't you have much more faith in ideas that you discover for yourself than in ideas that are handed to you on a silver platter? If so, isn't it bad judgment to try to ram your opinions down the throats of other people? Wouldn't it be wiser to make suggestions—and let the other man think out the conclusion for himself? Mr. Adolph Seltz of Philadelphia, a former student of mine, suddenly found himself confronted with the necessity of injecting enthusiasm into a discouraged and disorganized group of automobile salesmen. Calling a sales meeting, he urged his men to tell him exactly what they expected from him. As they talked, he wrote their ideas on the blackboard. He then said: "I'll give you all these qualities you expect from me. Now I want you to tell me what I have a right to expect from you." The replies came quick and fast. Loyalty. Honesty. Initiative. Optimism. Team work. Eight hours a day of enthusiastic work. One man volunteered to work fourteen hours a day. The meeting ended with a new courage, a new inspiration, and Mr. Seltz reported to me that the increase of sales had been phenomenal.

RULE NINE—*Be Sympathetic with the Other Person's Ideas and Desires*

Wouldn't you like to have a magic phrase that will stop argument, eliminate ill feeling, create good will and make the other person listen attentively? Yes? All right. Here it is. Begin by saying: "I don't blame you one iota for feeling as you do. If I were you, I should undoubtedly feel just as you do." An answer like that will soften the most cantankerous old cuss alive. And you can say that and be 100% sincere. Because if you were the other person, of course you would feel just as he does. Let me illustrate. Take Al Capone, for example. Suppose you had inherited the same body and temperament and mind that Al Capone inherited. Suppose you had had his environment and experiences. You would then be precisely what he is and where he is. For it is those things—and only those things—that made him what he is. The only reason, for example, that you are not a rattlesnake is because your mother and father weren't rattlesnakes. The only reason you don't kiss cows and consider snakes holy is because you weren't born in a Hindu family on the banks of the Brahmaputra. You deserve very little credit for being what you are—and remember, the man who comes to you irritated, bigoted, unreasoning, deserves very little discredit for being what he is. Feel sorry for the poor devil. Pity him. Sympathize with him. Say to yourself what John Wesley used to say when he saw a drunken bum staggering down the street: "There but for the grace of God, go I." Three-fourths of the people you will meet to-morrow are hungering and thirsting for sympathy. Give it to them, and they will love you.

To Reiterate:
Nine Ways to Help Win People to Your Way of Thinking

1. The only way to get the best of an argument is to avoid it.

2. Show respect for the other person's opinions. Never tell a man he is wrong.

3. If you are wrong, admit it quickly and emphatically.

4. Begin in a friendly way.

5. Get the other person saying "yes-yes" immediately.

6. Let the other man do a great deal of the talking.

7. Try honestly to see things from the other person's point of view.

8. Let the other man feel that the idea is his.

9. Be sympathetic with the other person's ideas and desires.

How to Win Friends and Influence People

This is a Condensation from Dale Carnegie's Best-Seller. The Complete Book is a Big Book of Thirty-Seven Chapters.

Including:

The Big Secret of Dealing with People

Six Ways to Make People Like You Instantly

An Easy Way to Become a Good Conversationalist

A Simple Way to Make a Good First Impression

How to Interest People

Twelve Ways to Win People to Your Way of Thinking

A Sure Way of Making Enemies—and How to Avoid It

The Safety Valve in Handling Complaints

How to Get Cooperation

A Formula That Will Work Wonders For You

The Movies Do It. Radio Does It. Why Don't You Do It?—

Nine Ways to Change People Without Giving Offense or Arousing Resentment

How to Criticize—and Not Be Hated for It

How to Spur Men on to Success

Making People Glad to Do What You Want

Letters That Produced Miraculous Results

Seven Rules for Making Home Life Happier

**We Have a
Book Recommendation for you**

The Dale Carnegie Course on Effective
Speaking, Personality Development, and
the Art of How to Win Friends & Influence
People By Dale Carnegie

Dale Carnegie's Radio Program: How to
Win Friends and Influence People - Lesson 1
by Dale Carnegie

The Power of Your Subconscious Mind by
Dr. Joseph Murphy

It Works by R. H. Jarrett

The Wisdom of Wallace D. Wattles - In-
cluding: The Science of Getting Rich, The
Science of Being Great & The Science of
Being Well By Wallace D. Wattles

The Dynamic Laws of Prosperity Series 3 :
Success is mental preparation by Catherine
Ponder

Warren Buffett Talks to MBA Students by
Warren Buffett

CPSIA information can be obtained at www.ICGtesting.com
Printed in the USA
LVOW041601141112

307323LV00004B/58/P